THE LITTLE BOOK OF

LOVE
SPELLS

THE LITTLE BOOK OF

LOVE SPELLS

SOPHIA

**Andrews McMeel
Publishing**

Kansas City

www.andrewsmcmeel.com

The Little Book of Love Spells is produced by becker&mayer!, Ltd.

ISBN: 0-8362-3261-5

Library of Congress Catalog Card Number: 97-71619

Edited by Alison Herschberg

02 TWP 10 9

ATTENTION: SCHOOLS AND BUSINESSES

Andrews McMeel books are available at quantity discounts with bulk purchase for educational, business, or sales promotional use. For information, please write to: Special Sales Department, Andrews McMeel Publishing, 4520 Main Street, Kansas City, Missouri 64111.

This book is dedicated to my loving, wonderful husband, Pan.

Introduction

What is love? Not puppy-dog, kitty-cat, best-friend-cute-baby love, but real, rip-roaring, red-hot, wild-about-you romantic love? Men can babble all they want (and they do) about pheromones, chemicals, breeding patterns, and instinct—we girls know better. Love is magic.

It may come and it may go, but when that magic spell of Big Love is working its charm, there's nothing like it. When love hits, you know it. You light up like a big bonfire and your heart dances like a flame. When that flame of passion dies down, some people may ask, "Where has the magic gone?" It hasn't gone anywhere. The magic of love is right here in your hands.

This book is a collection of my very best, old and new, tried-and-true love spells, and it is for all you women out there who value love. Why hope for that old romantic magic to just happen? With this book, girl, you can make it happen! Take control of your love life! People ask me: Are you serious? Are these real magic spells? Of course not! They are only for fun, enjoyment, amusement . . . unless, of course, they work!

In that case, well, I'll leave that up to you.

There are a few traditional sayings one should know about magic, whether you truly believe or not. First, "Watch out, you might get what you're after." This means think about what you're doing and look before you leap. The second is, "Don't call up what you can't put down." This means don't start what you don't intend to finish. And finally, "What goes around, comes around." Keeping these bits of advice in mind, love and love well! Have an adventurous heart and embrace life; have a blast and never sell yourself short. You deserve the best and—with this book—you're going to get it!

Finally, remember this advice: Stoke the embers of love every chance you get. Feed that fire, girl! Will that love to life! And toss an occasional firecracker in there to keep things lively!

Love, Sophia

Keep 'em Spellbound

He's got that deer-in-the-headlights look and you want to keep it that way. You have dazzled him and snared him, and he's seeing nothing but stars. You want to keep that silly grin on his fixated face—and here's how to do it.

You Will Need
+ salt
+ three cords, about a foot in length—one red, one black, one white (Leather is best, but anything will do.)

The Spell
At dusk when the moon is almost full, sprinkle some salt over the cords and yourself, saying:

CLEAN OF THOUGHT, CLEAN OF DEED.
MY THOUGHTS AND WORDS YOU WILL NOW HEED.

Hold up the white, red, and black cords in turn,
visualize them glowing with energy, and say:

WHITE, WHITE,
IN ME SEE LIGHT.
BE IT DAY OR BE IT NIGHT,
I AM ALWAYS IN YOUR SIGHT!

RED, RED, I FILL YOUR HEAD.
OURS A RED-HOT BURNING BED.
BE IT DAY OR BE IT NIGHT,
I AM ALWAYS FILLED WITH MIGHT!

BLACK, BLACK, I COVER YOUR BACK,
IN THE DREAMTIME, IN THE SEA TIME.

BE IT DAY OR BE IT NIGHT,
YOU ARE PULLED INTO MY FLIGHT!

Now braid the cords together, tying knots at each end.
Make it look nice, saying:

RED, BLACK, WHITE,
ALL IS FILLED WITH LIGHT,
I BRING YOU DELIGHT!
SHRI!

Later, give it to him as a gift—a wristband or a necklace. If he's
not the accessories type, at least make him try it on. You
should tie it onto his body yourself, if possible. If he won't
wear it, make him promise to save it as a keepsake . . . zap!

To Bring a Special Spark to a Date

Some dates are boring, some dates are fun. Some dates,
however, are just waiting for that right spark to make them
truly passionate. What are *you* waiting for?
Toss that match in and see what happens . . .

You Will Need
+ red lipstick
+ rose oil

The Spell
Before your date, put on the red lipstick. Dab some oil
on your temples and chest, saying:

From seed to bud,
Root to flower,
As a rose I open to the sun.
As all shall open to my power!

Touch a dab of the oil onto your lips, press them together,
and smile. Visualize yourself as a bright red rose opening,
and strut on out.

To Catch the Eye of Another

You can't keep your eyes off him, so why doesn't he glance back at you? You are royal and deserving! He should at least have the decency to return the look—and then some! This'll turn his head.

You Will Need
+ a real crystal, preferably on an earring

The Spell
At the full moon, go outside somewhere quiet and wild. Hold the crystal to the full-moon light. Then say:

> Mater luna, burning bright,
> Fill this gem with thy might.

AS YOU CATCH THE HIDDEN LIGHT,
MAY I SHINE AND CATCH HIS SIGHT!
LUNA LUX!

Wear the crystal when you're around him, and don't
forget to smile when you slide up to him and say,
"Take a picture, it'll last longer!"

Turning Up the Heat of Love

Okay, you've dated, had fun, established that you have shared
interests, yak, yak, yak. You're ready to shift into a higher gear,
but he's still cruising. It's time to slowly and craftily
turn up the temperature . . . *sssssss!*

You Will Need
+ some cayenne pepper in a small cup
+ a red flower of your choice

The Spell
At sunset before he comes over, take some of the pepper from
the cup and sprinkle a pinch of it around you while saying:

> Heat of earth,
> Red of love,

Come from below,
Come from above.

Hold the rest of the cayenne pepper and the flower above
your head. Close your eyes and visualize them surrounded
by red flames of love. Then say:

Flames of love rise up!
Pyre of joy rise higher!
Come my love and we will fly,
On red wings of pure desire!
Sa!

Later in the evening, slip some of the cayenne pepper into
dinner, drinks, dip, etc. Wear the red flower behind your ear.
You will know the spell has succeeded when he pulls you close
to him and drops the flower onto the floor.

9

"She's Gotta Have It" Spell

You just spied him across the dance floor—cute beyond words
with a tight butt in blue jeans. He is every cowgirl's dream.
Nothing can stop you. . . . You have to have his boots under
your bed tonight! Here's how to do it.

You Will Need
+ civet oil (synthetic please)

You are about to invoke the magic of the Egyptian cat goddess,
Bast, the goddess of love and desire. Conjure up the image of
yourself as a sleek cat, and your object of desire as the mouse.
Cats love to play with their food before devouring it. Looking
at him very kitty-like, whisper:

BAST, GODDESS OF LOVE, CAT OF DESIRE,
COME IGNITE THE SACRED FIRE!
FILL ME NOW . . . WITH
MEOW!

Put the civet oil on and slink on over. Pounce on him and purr.

Glamour-Puss Glamour Spell

You're slumming. Relaxing. Letting your normal ultra-glamorous, gorgeous, and gifted persona slip for a while. In short, you look like hell. Suddenly, he shows up. *Panic!* This spell will cause you to look casual and cute as opposed to a disheveled wreck.

You Will Need
+ a little rosemary (fresh is best)
+ some water
+ a mirror

The Spell
Before you engage your uninvited guest in casual conversation, excuse yourself for a moment. Mix some of the rosemary into the water while saying:

ROSEMARY, ROSEMARY HELP THOU ME.
FROM ALL SHADOWS MAKE ME FREE.
CAST ME IN THE FINEST LIGHT,
TO BE LOVELY IN ALL SIGHT!

Wash your face with clean water from the tap. Sprinkle the
rosemary water all about you and look in the mirror, saying:

SWEET AND FRESH AND PURE AND FAIR,
ALL MADE BEAUTIFUL BY SCENTED AIR,
GLOOM AND SORROW WASHED AWAY,
ALL WHO COME WILL LOVE ME TODAY!

Dry yourself off and throw on something halfway decent.
Crush the remaining rosemary in your hands and breathe in
the scent deeply. Now go out and knock him dead.

TUG 'EM BACK SPELL

Everything is going smoothly. He buys the flowers at the right
time, he's a tiger when you want one and a pussycat when you
change your mind. But he has roving eyes. No cause for alarm . . .
yet. This spell will put your mind at rest by rotating his gaze
back where it belongs—fixed on your glorious self!

YOU WILL NEED
+ a lemon
+ a tiger-eye (optional)

THE SPELL
Cut open the lemon. With your finger, take some juice
and draw an eye on your chest. (You can also use a tiger-eye to
draw on the lemon.) Visualize this eye glowing on
your heart, saying:

I AM THE EYE AND YOU MUST SEE,
ALL THE LOVELINESS THAT IS ME.
LOVELY, LOVELY I SHALL BE.

FROM THIS EYE YOU ARE NOT FREE,
BY MY HEART WHICH YOU CAN SEE,
ALWAYS ALWAYS LOOK ONLY AT ME!

Bite into the lemon and put a little juice on your hands
and temples. If you have it, slip the tiger-eye into your bra.
When you see him and he looks at your chest, visualize
your heart-eye glowing, capturing his attention—
then kiss him really hard. Got 'em!

THE COLD SHOWER SPELL

He's hot—on you, that is. You like him, but you could use a little
breathing room. He needs to hit the breaks a bit, but you don't
want him to vanish, just . . . cool it. This'll do it.

YOU WILL NEED
+ a piece of red paper
+ a pen
+ a paper cup

THE SPELL

On the piece of red paper, write all the over-the-top, lovey-
dovey stuff he's said to you. (A particularly gooey example might
be, "We are soul mates. I need you this lifetime.") Then say:

FIRE FALLS FROM YOUR TONGUE,
LOVE WHOSE PACE IS HOT.

ON ME YOUR LOVE IS HUNG,
NOW IT'S GROWING, SOON IT'S NOT!

Fold the piece of paper into a triangle, and shove it into
the paper cup. Fill the cup with water and put it into
your freezer, saying:

BE YOU YOUNG, BE YOU OLD,
YOU BE CHILL, YOU BE COLD.
STILL WITHIN THE FIRE BURNS.
OUR LOVE IS FINE, IT SHALL NOT TURN.
"CHILL OUT, GUY." (OR SOMETHING SIMILAR.)

Shut the freezer door. If you want the relationship to heat up,
simply take the cup out of the freezer,
dry the paper and burn it, and say:

NOW IT'S GROWING, SOON IT'S HOT! HOT, HOT!

Watch the flames grow!

"Kiss Me You Fool!" Spell

He's fun, you have a great time, and you're starting to click.
So when will he kiss you? You vote *now!* Not little pecks on the
cheek—we're talking about a big, wet, wild kiss. Maybe he's getting
over an ex—burned in love—but who cares!? This will get him to
make the leap, and he will be oh-so-very-glad he did.

You Will Need
+ red wine (or juice)
+ two nice glasses
+ a red rose
+ gardenia oil

The Spell
Before your date with the chosen one,
pour the wine or juice into the glasses, saying:

YOU WILL FIND ME FAIR, FAIR, FAIR . . .

Draw a circle about you with the rose, saying:

DESIRE FILLS THE AIR, AIR, AIR . . .

Put the gardenia oil on as a perfume, saying:

KISS ME IF YOU CARE, CARE, CARE!!!

Then put the glasses in the refrigerator. When you see him later that night, give him one of the glasses and the rose, and say something like, "Do you have anything for me?" Then melt!

Old Dog, New Tricks Spell

How long have you two been together—not counting the dating, living together, engagement, and now marriage? Has it been a while since that wildfire burned bright? Has it lost that spark? Never fear! Yes, you *can* teach an old dog new tricks.

You Will Need
+ black lingerie
+ a yellow candle

The Spell

Take out your new black lingerie and rub it on the candle, thinking lewd thoughts. Then say these words:

Our love has grown, our love is strong.
The spark's died down and that is wrong.

AGAIN LIKE NEW LOVE IT WILL BE,
NEW JOY AND LUST IMMEDIATELY!

When he's home, put on the lingerie, light the candle, and say:

OUR LOVE GROWS STRONGER
AS THE FLAME GROWS LONGER!

Now, go fetch that old dog and give him a bone.

Clean Up His Act Spell

He just doesn't care enough about appearances. Maybe it's
dirty fingernails and hair, or maybe he is just a slob. If he
always looks like he just got out of bed, do not despair!
It's nothing a little spell won't cure!

You Will Need
+ a new hairbrush
+ a piece of white cord

The Spell

Hold the bristle part of the brush while wrapping the cord
around the handle. Visualize your man cleaning up his act
once and for all and enjoying being well-scrubbed.
As you are wrapping the brush with the cord, say:

I bind you clean,
I bind you fine,
From head to toes,
You'll wear nice clothes.
You are mine!
You are mine!

Repeat these same words over and over until you are done
wrapping the brush. When the handle is wrapped, hide it in
your sock drawer until your love-slob comes over. Then
romantically brush his hair for him, slowly, sexily telling him
how much better he'd look if he would only. . . . Then see the
change. No more five o'clock shadow, no more raggedy
hand-me-downs. Repeat as necessary, and for goodness'
sake, take that poor man shopping!

"One-Night Stand" Spell

You see him, he sees you—zap! The electricity flies between you. It's not true love, it isn't the warm glow of friendship. You know what that feeling is and you want some *now!* Here's how to hook him fast and hard, if only for one night. But as we all know, a night can last forever . . . this'll make sure it does. It'll also make sure he doesn't wear out his welcome.

You Will Need
+ a small vial of musk oil

The Spell
Before you leave for your night on the town, be sure you've got your vial of oil. When your eyes meet, put some oil slowly on your neck and wrists. Stare at him and smile just a little, then tap out this rhythm with your right hand on your thigh (practice first):

Dum-da-dum-dum (long-short-long-long)
Dum-da-dum-dum
Dum-da-dum-dum

As you do this, in your mind hear these words
echo with the beat:

Come to me now
Come to me now
Come to me now

He will come over, and when he does, make sure you manage
to rub one of your musk-scented wrists on him. As you do this,
hear the following words in your mind:

You are mine now
You are mine now
You are mine now

He's hooked! Reel him in, take him home!
Cook him any way you want!

Just One Look (But You Want Another) Spell

It was a casual meeting, but you both felt the chemistry—you were just a little too shy to introduce yourselves. "Ships in the night" is not what you want this to turn out to be. What if you never see each other again? You'll wonder what would have happened if you'd only. . . . Want to meet again and check each other out? Forget those "I saw you" ads! This is what you do.

You Will Need
+ a regular deck of cards
+ salt

The Spell

Take the deck of cards and remove the king, queen, and five of hearts. At midnight, after a new moon, place the five of hearts

over the king and queen. Take a small amount of salt and
throw pinches to the four directions. Say this as you
throw the salt:

On the earth
He does roam.
Bring me to him,
Bring me home,
It is meant to be
He will come to me!
Five of hearts
Make him see!

Leave the cards like that in a place they will not be disturbed.

You will meet each other again by the next full moon,
only this time it will not be by accident!

COME-HITHER SPELL

You see him, he sees you. You orbit near each other but,
it seems, in different solar systems. You want him to edge a
bit closer, strike up a real conversation, show some interest.
Adjust his orbit so you two can get to know each other—
this spell will swing his star closer.

YOU WILL NEED

+ some red thread
+ a small stone that you find with a natural hole in it
(Stones like this are very powerful.)

THE SPELL

Cut of a piece of thread three feet long. Tie one end of the
thread through the hole in your rock, making a pendulum. At
midnight on the next full moon, go outside and hold the stone
so you can see the moon through the hole. Say:

(DESIRED PERSON'S NAME)
I FEEL YOU THROUGH THE MOON,
COME NOW CLOSER
YOU WILL SOON!

Now, holding the string, swing the stone slowly about your head like an orbiting moon, saying three times:

☉ DIANA, ARIADNE
DRAWN TO ME
HE WILL BE!

While reciting these words, let the thread wrap around your finger as the stone spins. Keep spinning the stone so that its orbit gets smaller and smaller with each turn, until the spinning ends with the stone in your hand. Stand for a moment in silence, then bury the stone at the foot of a willow tree, saying:

(NAME)
FLY THROUGH THE MOON.
COME NOW CLOSER
YOU WILL SOON!

The Spicy Root of Seduction Spell

It's simple. You know that you want him, and you know that he wants you. But maybe he doesn't *realize* that he wants you. So the plan of attack is to seduce! This spell will give the seduction a real power charge and get you where you want to go.

You Will Need
+ ginger root
+a nice bottle of red wine

The Spell
Enter the arena of seduction. Place a piece of the ginger root in the room, and put a small piece in the bottle of red wine, saying:

> I want you, I want you.
> Feel it too, feel it too.

LUST AND LIGHT
FEEL IT TONIGHT!

Turn the heat up. As the night progresses, serve the wine, silently saying to yourself the same chant as before. Visualize your desire as glowing red light, and see the red light of your desire enter him as he drinks the wine. See it fill him. Then have him pour you a glass. Hold it up to the light and say:

BEAUTIFUL RED LIGHT, ISN'T IT?

Then drink, and feel his red light of desire enter you. Sit close to him, feeling the red light within you and within him blend together. He is pulled to you by the heat . . .

Love Me Forever Spell

Love is as fickle as a cat. You've got a hot love going—adoration, great times, maybe even a bit of (gasp!) commitment! Things are going grandly and will probably continue to do so. But . . . will it last forever? This spell is a little insurance, honey.

You Will Need

◆ two previously worn "love items"—one yours, one his
◆ a small stick cut from an oak tree
(Cut it when the moon is waxing—getting bigger.)
◆ a two-foot strand of freshly cut ivy
(also cut when the moon is waxing)

The Spell

Pick a day that is special to your relationship. At noon, tie the two love items around the stick, using the ivy to wrap everything together. Leave a little ivy at the end, which you will wrap later. As you do this, say:

> YOU'RE BOUND TO ME
> AND I TO THEE.
> WE TWO SEEDS
> ARE NOW ONE TREE.
> NOW AND FOREVER,
> SO MAY IT BE!

Hide the bundle under your bed until midnight. Then take it out again and finish wrapping the bundle completely, saying:

> I AM BOUND TO THEE
> AND YOU TO ME.
> TOGETHER DIVINE
> WE ARE ONE VINE.
> NOW AND FOREVER,
> SO MAY IT BE!

Keep the bundle under your bed and make love as soon as possible. When you do so, visualize you and your lover as two vines, or trees, growing together. Later, plant the bundle in a patch of ivy. Your love will remain firm.

I'm the Boss
(and Don't Forget It) Spell

When you are in love, but need to reassert your primacy over your
mate, you can pound your chest and pounce on him—or try this.

You Will Need

✦ a nice artistic rod, staff, or club (bought or handmade).
(Something from another culture is best—and easier to pass off
as a unique decoration—which it isn't, as you'll soon see.)

The Spell

At noon on a very sunny day, take the rod with you to a
high place and raise it to the sun, saying:

Force and power,
Lion's roar,
Magma to solar,

WINGED FIRE SOAR!
TYR!

Visualize the staff burning with energy like a shooting arrow, and then bring it back to your den, office, or any place you are likely to encounter your loved one. When your *amour* enters, show the staff to him. At an appropriate moment, pound it on the floor or a table at least once, "to show him how solid it is" (or something like that).

Now, look him right in the eyes and feel the force of the sun flow from the rod through you, through your eyes, and to him. He is seeing you filled with power, huge, overpowering. . . . At this moment, step forward with the rod until he moves back a step, then point it at him (like you're showing it off) and say, "See?" Then suddenly excuse yourself and go; look at a clock and make some excuse.

Hang the rod up as you go out, leaving the poor dazed guy to try and figure out what happened. Use that rod from now on to reassert control. . . . Use your imagination.

Nip It in the Bud

He was an interesting guy. It looked promising but, well . . .
you've decided to pass. Let's make this easy for everyone:
You go your way, and this spell will send him (even if he is
infatuated), gently and respectfully, on his way. *C'est la vie* . . .

You Will Need
+ some kind of paper token from the rejected one
(or something of his attached to a piece of paper)
+ a new penny
+ a small, watertight container

The Spell
Make a small paper boat out of the paper. At sunset, take the
boat to a stream or brook. Pause at the water's edge and say:

FLOW AWAY, FLY AWAY,
GO AWAY, GLIDE AWAY.
WHAT WAS CHANCED
CAN NOT LAST.
SAIL FROM THE PRESENT
INTO THE PAST!
FIAT!

Take the penny, whisper good-bye to the person, and tuck
the penny into the boat. Send it floating away.

Take a little of the river water home with you in your container
and sprinkle it around your house. He is gone.

A Spell to Get a "Body Buddy"

There are times when you just want to have fun with someone.
Body fun. No long-term plans, no deep connections, only a
mutually physically satisfying relationship tied together with a
friendship. Why not? This spell will attract just the type of
hunk you want with no deep, potential entanglements.

You Will Need
+ a large pin
+ two candles—one white and one red

The Spell
Stick the pin through the white candle horizontally all the
way, so it sticks out the other end. On the full moon, dance
naked and think wild thoughts. Think of the type of man you
want to attract, think of the fun you'll have! Take the red
candle and rub it on your body, saying:

BODY TO BODY, BLOOD TO BLOOD,
FIRE TO FIRE, FLOOD TO FLOOD.

Light the red candle, saying:

BRING THE BODY, BRING THE FLESH.
LET US MINGLE, LET US MESH.

Then push the two candles together, the pin from the white
candle piercing the red one, until they are joined, side by side.
Then say again:

BRING THE BODY, BRING THE FLESH.
LET US MINGLE, LET US MESH.

Then, lighting the wick of the white candle from the
already burning red one, say a third time:

BRING THE BODY, BRING THE FLESH.
LET US MINGLE, LET US MESH!

Clap your hands three times, saying:

AMAT! AMAT! AMAT!

Let the candles burn down together completely, watching
carefully. You will soon meet your body buddy and sparks
will fly . . . but don't expect marriage!

Talk Dirty to Me Spell

Grrrrr. Dirty words, erotic thoughts, sexy ideas . . . these are a
few of your favorite things. Once in a while, it is great to get
wild and very verbal. After all, the dirtiest organ of the body is
the brain—why not put it to good use? This is primarily a
phone spell, but with a little improvisation (and a few scarves),
it could easily become a parlor game.

You Will Need
+ three red candles
+ proximity to a phone
+ a lavender stalk
+ matches

The Spell
Place the candles about the phone so they make a

point-up triangle. Lay the lavender stalk horizontally
across the phone, saying:

SPIRIT OF SOUND, SPIRIT OF WORD.
HEAR MY VOICE, I AM NOW HEARD.
EROS OF TOUCH, EROS OF NEED,
COME FORTH AS WORDS!
THIS IS MY NEED!

Then call him or wait for his call. As you're talking, light the
lavender and circle yourself with the scented smoke. Then,
innocently, steer the conversation into the erotic end zone and
light one candle, saying into the phone:

HOW HOT ARE YOU?
HOW HOT ARE YOU?
TELL ME NOW AND TELL ME TRUE.
WHAT DO YOU LIKE, WHAT WOULD YOU DO?

If he doesn't get it, explain that it's a game and that one candle is lit—two to go. Get him talking dirty, goad him, push him, tease him, whisper to him . . . then say the chant again and light the second candle.

Push it further. The vibe will get him, don't worry. Light the third candle, then repeat the verse. Look out! Try not to burn up the phone lines or blow an electrical fuse!

When done, blow out all the candles and say:

GONE WITH THE SMOKE,
FILLED WITH THE FIRE,
MAY OUR LOVE GROW,
LIKE A SAPPHIRE!
EROS!

Spell to Cause a Little Change

You love your sweetie, but sometimes you think that just a little change in his habits or character would make him ever so much better—"icing on the cake," if you will. Well, no one is perfect (at least not as close to perfect as you are), but people can certainly be improved with just a little psychic effort. All you have to do is use this little spell.

You Will Need
+ a knife (Silver is best, but any will do.)
+ a stick of cinnamon bark

The Spell
One week before the new moon, take the knife and cinnamon bark to a quiet place and say:

WOOD OF HERMES, BLADE OF MOON.
BY OUR LOVE GRANT THIS BOON.
CAUDACUS!

Then, using the knife to scratch the cinnamon, carve the name
of the little foible of his you wish to banish or change. For
example, "Keep the lid down." When possible, save the
cinnamon scratchings, as you will place them in something he
will eat or drink. As you add the scratchings to something he
will consume, burn a little of the cinnamon stick, visualizing
the intended change, and say:

CHANGE IS GROWTH, CHANGE IS GOOD,
BY THE BLADE, BY THE ROOD.
WITH LOVE I TOSS, WITH LOVE I CAST,
HERE NO LOSS, CHANGE WILL LAST!
MUTENSIA!

Then bury the remains of the burned cinnamon stick.
By the new moon, that change will unfold.

A Spell to Make the Nice Guy a Little Nastier

A lot of men just don't get it. Why do women fall for jerks? Is it because they are so great? Not exactly. It's just that it's hard to really get into a lover who is *always* nice, right? Without a touch of macho/jerk/warrior, a guy is just, well, a wimp. If your sweetheart is just a bit too sweet, try a little of this.

You Will Need
+ some iron nails
+ a metal pot
+ a cup of vinegar

The Spell
On a sunny day, take the iron nails and place them in the metal pot with the vinegar. At noon, bring it all to a boil, saying:

By the thorn, by the blade,
Strength is born, force is made!

Place the hot pot out into the sunlight to cool
and absorb the sun's energy, saying:

By the fire, by the sun,
Full of desire, full of fun!

Later, strain the liquid into a container and
bury the nails at the base of a mighty tree (oak is best).
Add the potion to his bathwater, saying:

What is soft, now grows strong.
What is small, now grows long.
Vita! Vita! Vita!

Make sure he soaks, then dry him off. He'll be a better man for it.
Repeat when his voltage runs low.

A Spontaneous Spell

He plans and plans, and he does it so well! This time, this place, this party, these friends, at that time . . . Wouldn't just a*little* chaos be good? How about some spontaneity? Some of the great mind-blowing moments arise without a plan except joy. This will spark a little love explosion.

You Will Need
+ some natural vanilla oil
+ a sparkler (the kind you light)
+ matches

The Spell
On the first day of a new moon, rub the oil over the sparkler, then spin it about the room, saying:

WHAT IS STATIC, NOW MUST CHURN.
WHAT IS SOLID, MUST NOW BURN!
LOOSEN UP, SHAKE UP,
TURN WHEEL, TURN!

Later, at night, hold the sparkler hidden when you are
out with him and whisper:

LOOSEN UP, SHAKE IT!
JOYFUL JOY MAKE IT!

Pull it out and light it. As his mouth falls open, dance about
him with the sparkler. Make him laugh. When it's done, kiss
him. Let the smoke drift over you and enjoy the new sparks.

The Fetch Spell

We have all been told a thousand times that men are hunters, they must seek out and kill, bring home the mastodon—or whatever. But what about when they get a remote control in their hands? Or, heaven forbid, a cellular phone? Men just don't fetch like they used to. You rarely see them bringing home the spoils of conquest: roses, chocolate, or even getting up to make coffee in the early morning. This little spell will have him waiting on you a bit more like the princess you are.

You Will Need

✦ a little pollen from any flower (Or you can get a little from a health-food store if none is available outside.)

The Spell

Holding the pollen in your hands, walk around the outside of your home (clockwise), and then enter the door, saying several times:

AROUND AND AROUND, RICHES ABOUND.
BRING WHAT YOU SEE, BRING IT TO ME!

Later that night, place a pinch of pollen
in each of his shoes, saying:

BRING WHAT YOU SEE, BRING IT TO ME.
I AM THE QUEEN, YOU ARE THE BEE.
AS I DESIRE, SO SHALL IT BE!

You can imagine all the neat stuff he'll "think of" to do for—or
bring to—you. After you've put the pollen in his shoes, mix the
rest of the pollen into some hot water and drink it, saying:

AROUND AND AROUND, RICHES ABOUND.
YOU ARE FREE, BRING ALL TO ME!
AS I DESIRE, SO SHALL IT BE!

A Spell to Make 'em Come Back for More

Hey, was that date fun, or was it *fun* ? Girl, your head is still spinning. It could be love, but you'll never know unless he asks you out again. There are more kinds of baits to trap that bear into another date than you can imagine. This little number should do it.

You Will Need
+ a very clean wishbone from a chicken
+ some green thread
+ something he touched or owns

The Spell
Tie the top of the wishbone to his personal
object with the thread, saying:

Found, bound, to me, quickly, so may it be!

YOU I FOUND,
YOU I BOUND,
FLY TO ME,
COME QUICKLY!
FUGIAT!

Visualize him calling you, returning to you, and place the little bundle in your bed. Sleep with it for three days, each day rubbing the bone and saying:

He will either come to you within those three days or it was never meant to be. Either way, after three days have passed, bury the item (with salt if he never returned).

THE SPELL OF THE WILD POWER BED

The shared bed. Is any place more special? It's a sanctuary, a passion pit, a temple of love, and a home entertainment center. Want to liven up your bed? Zap it with that special *love* vibe! Here is an easy way to make that bed oh-so-much-more than a set of springs!

YOU WILL NEED

> + some salt
> + rose oil
> + seven cloves

THE SPELL

On the full moon, wash your sheets and pillowcases with a little soap and some salt. When they are completely clean, run them through again with no soap. When the machine is full of water, add some of the rose oil and say:

> BUD COME TO BLOOM,
> BED FILL MY ROOM,

LOVE-FILLED FLOWER,
BED FILL WITH POWER!

Then add the seven cloves and say:

CLOVES FILL WITH MIGHT,
MY BED OF DELIGHT,
ENERGY-FILLED FLOWER,
BED FILL WITH POWER!

While the sheets are washing, sprinkle the bare bed with salt,
then sweep it clean. Dry the sheets, put them on the bed,
leap on it naked, and say:

FLESH THIS SPELL,
EMPOWER IT WELL!
JOY-FILLED FLOWER,
THIS BED IS POWER!
AWOOOOOOOOOOOOOOOOOO!

Look out world, her highness has found her throne!
All bow before the queen!

Get What You Want
(How to Attract a Dream Lover)

Sigh. Another trashy romance novel finished, yet no dashing young hero has entered your life—at least, not lately. Instead of pining away for that oh-so-perfect, romantic, adventurous, tough (yet tender) dream lover, make it happen and make him real! Dreams do come true, it could happen to you.

You Will Need
+ a piece of purple paper
+ a pink pen
+ a small cloth bag
+ some lavender

THE SPELL

At midnight on a romantic night or when a new crescent moon
is in the sky, take the piece of purple paper and write all the
attributes you want your dream lover to possess. Should he be
strong? Handsome? Rich? It's up to you. When you are done,
draw a big crescent moon over your writing, and say:

> I SEE YOU CLEAR,
> I SEE YOU HERE,
> I'M IN YOUR ARMS
> WITHOUT FEAR.
> BY THE MOON, THE STARS, AND SKY.
> INTO YOUR ARMS
> I WILL FLY.

Roll up the paper and put it in the cloth bag with the lavender.
Tie off one end and hold it to your heart, saying:

I conjure thee, I conjure thee,
Oh, dream lover
Let me see.
In my dreams you will be,
Reveal your true face to me.
Luna amor!

Place the bag under your pillow and fantasize about this
dream lover as you fall asleep. You will dream of your dream
lover coming to you. He may be a little different from what
you expect, but you should embrace him. If you can hold
him tight in your dream, he will soon appear in your life
when you are awake. Keep trying!

Owner/Slave Spell

Love is about power and power is about love. Sometimes
you simply must have the upper hand. So what if you're
controlling? Is there a problem with that? I don't *think* so!
When you have to take the bull by the horns (i.e., get a
lover under your thumb), try this tasty little spell.

You Will Need
+ a black licorice whip
+ a picture of the "victim"
+ a sterilized pin

The Spell
At midnight, face north and hold the licorice in your left
hand and the picture in your right hand. Say:

POWER OF EARTH, ROOT, AND STONE,
FILL ME WITH POWER
I AM ALONE.
NOW IS THE HOUR, LET IT BE DONE.
I AM THE RULER!
I AM THE ONE!

Prick your finger with the pin and put some blood on
both the picture and the licorice stick, saying:

POWER OF LIFE, POWER OF FIRE,
I FILL HIM NOW WITH MY DESIRE.
ABOVE HIM I STAND, PLACE ME HIGHER.
NOW IS THE HOUR, LET IT BE DONE.
I AM THE RULER!
I AM THE ONE!

Tie the licorice about the picture and say:

> BOUND TO ME YOU NOW SHALL BE.
> UNTIL I DEEM TO SET YOU FREE.
> AS I WILL, SO SHALL IT BE.
> NOW IS THE HOUR, LET IT BE DONE.
> I AM THE RULER!
> I AM THE ONE!

Leave the licorice in your bed or in a drawer. The next time he comes over, slyly untie the licorice in secret and get him to eat at least some of it. As he does, visualize the licorice as a leash in your hand and around his neck. Smile. Next time you want him to do something, take out his picture and command him. When you see him, whatever you request, he'll do. *Be nice!*

Dance with Me

Sometimes you just want to go out and get wild, get down, rock 'n' roll, do the two-step, or trip the dance fantastic, right? And the very worst thing is getting asked to dance by creeps, sloppy toe-stomping drunks, and other assorted losers. This little spell will attract the right dance partners. Then? Who knows . . .

You Will Need
- ✦ two dimes
- ✦ a knife

The Spell
Before you go out dancing, take the two dimes and put them down on a flat surface. Turn one faceup and the other face-down. Put your right hand on the dime that is faceup and your left on the dime that is facedown. Then say:

COME TO THE DANCE,
BRING ROMANCE.
JOYFUL DANCER,
COME TO ME!
AWFUL PRANCER
LET ME BE!

Taking the knife, cut an ✕ in the dime that is facedown.
"Drill" a point into the dime that is faceup. Tap the faceup
coin with the knife and say:

COME WHEN I TAP,
GREAT MAN OF FUN!

Tap the facedown coin with the knife, and say:

BE GONE WHEN I TAP,
EVIL MAN RUN!

> DANCE, DANCE,
> I INVOKE ROMANCE!
> GOOD PARTNERS TO ME,
> ALL ELSE FLEE!

Place the faceup coin carefully into your right shoe or boot
(faceup), then place the facedown coin just as carefully into
your left shoe or boot. Then, yeeeeeee ha! Go dancing! When
you need a cool dance partner, tap your right foot and say:

> COME WHEN TAP,
> GREAT MAN OF FUN!

If a jerk approaches, tap the left foot and say:

> BEGONE WHEN I TAP,
> EVIL MAN RUN!

The spell only works for one night—but oh
what a night it will be!

Love Is in the Air

You like him. Now you want to slowly pull him into your world. Like urging him into your pool of love—maybe you just want him to dip his feet, maybe you want him to dive in. In any event, simply putting out the right vibe can accomplish whatever sweet designs you might have. A simple stick of incense can make the difference between a lifelong love and a casual friend. Light 'em up, girl!

You Will Need

+ one lily (yellow for friendship; orange, pink, or red for passion)
+ a stick of incense (sandalwood for slow friendship and first attraction, musk for heavy-duty, all-out passion)

The Spell

On or near the full moon, invite him over to your place. Before he comes, place the lily in a vase in the center of the room , saying:

> HERE THE HEARTH, HERE THE HOME!
> FLOWER OF ATTRACTION,
> CENTER OF MY HEART,
> IN THOUGHT,
> WORD, AND ACTION,
> PADMA!

Take the incense stick and point it to the
four directions, each time saying:

> WINDS OF THE CORNER,
> WINDS OF POWER,
> FILL MY HOME
> WITH WINDS OF DESIRE!

Hold the incense above the lily and light it, then waltz
clockwise around your house, saying:

BREATH OF KAMA, BREATH OF LOVE,
FLOW THROUGH THE AIR
FROM HEAVEN ABOVE.

Then place the incense in the vase with the flower and say:

SYLPHS AND SPIRITS OF LOVE AND TRUST,
FILL NOW MY HOME, COME NOW, YOU MUST!

Let the incense burn out. Relax and sip a warm drink until he
arrives. Poor guy, he won't know what hit him!

To Reunite Old Lovers

Nothing burns like an old flame. Okay, maybe there was a
reason (or two) that you two broke up—but hindsight is
golden, and mmm, mmm, he sure looks good right now.
Want to rekindle a romance once thought to be extinct?
Well, before attempting to reconnect, do this little number,
and all will click like it used to.

You Will Need

✦ two small birthday candles
(one gold or yellow and one silver or white)

The Spell

On a nice day, when both the sun and the moon are in the sky
(usually late afternoon), go outside with the candles
and look at the sun and moon.

Light the gold candle and hold it up to the sun, saying:

Sun of gold,
As you burn,
Man of mine,
Soon return.

Light the silver candle and hold it up to the moon, saying:

Moon of silver,
I who yearn,
Moon to sun,
To you I turn.

Slowly bring the candles together, side by side, saying:

Old, old flame; new, new flame.
Gone is sorrow, gone is blame.
What was undone, again has begun.
Two were split, again are one!
Heiros gamos!

Let the two candles burn down together, mixing and melting.
Close your eyes. Clearly see yourself getting back together with
him again. When they burn out, go make that call!

Commitment Spell

You and your sweetie have a good thing going. You snuggle for
hours, you are together a whole lot, and relationship-wise
things are going well. But . . . you want that little extra commitment. Maybe you want a ring, maybe just a very sincere
promise backed up by an apartment lease (get the ring!), but
whatever form it may take, you want something more than just
a "let's see how things go." This spell will get that boy off his
butt without rocking the boat.

You Will Need

+ a patch of ivy or some other lovely vine
(one that will not be uprooted!)
+ some shower water from him and from you
(gathered discreetly), in two different bottles

THE SPELL

The day after the new moon, go to the vine patch in the early morning and find two strands of vine that are growing next to each other. Carefully untangle them so you are holding both strands.

Splash some of "his" water on one strand, and say:

HERE HE'S ROOTED, HERE HE'LL STAY.
ABIDING WITH ME NEVER GOING AWAY!
GREEN MAN (HIS NAME)!

Splash some of "your" water on the other strand of ivy and say:

HERE I AM ROOTED, HERE I WILL STAY.
TOGETHER WITH HIM FOREVER I SAY.
GREEN WOMAN (YOUR NAME)!

Pour the rest of all the water on the roots of the vine. Then carefully twist the strands together clockwise, saying:

Bound together never apart.
Bound to the end right from the start.
Commit to me, I commit to thee.
Our love is one,
So mote it be!

Silently leave and let the vines grow together. By the next new moon you will get a commitment pledge of some kind from your beloved.

Getting a Rich Man Spell

We all know that money can't buy love, love is more precious
than gold, and rich men are not always loving men . . . but it
could happen! Why can't he be cute, nice, and—dare I say it—
loaded? Fishing for a rich lover takes a little research, some
nerve, a lot of determination, and this little spell to project
the vibe. Put on your best outfit, dab on that expensive
perfume, wear your best jewelry, scatter money all over
the room, and then do this:

You Will Need
+ a thin, medium-sized green candle
+ a candleholder
+ a red pen
+ a little salt
+ a new dollar bill

THE SPELL

First, set up the candle (unlit) in the candleholder, and place
the pen in the center of the room. Scatter the salt about the
room counterclockwise, and visualize all debts and bills flying
away! Then take up the new dollar bill.

Dance clockwise about the candle, saying:

> MONEY COME IN,
> CARRY IN HIM
> WHO BRINGS ME GOLD,
> THAT NEVER GROWS OLD!
> SA, SA, SA!

On the dollar, carefully write the specific things you want from
your rich guy, whether you have someone in mind or not.
(For example: *rich, wealthy, loaded, etc.*)

When done, wrap the dollar bill around the candle.
Use a lit match to melt a little wax off the candle to "glue" the
dollar to it. Then hold the candle tightly to your perfumed,
bejeweled chest and say:

LIKE A BEE TO A FLOWER,
I ATTRACT MONEY POWER.
POUR ON ME
SWEET MONEY,
I PULL HIM NOW
INTO MY BOWER!
SA, SA, SA!

Place the candle back into the candleholder, light it, and relax.
Keep an eye on it as it burns down. When it hits the dollar it
will burn fast. When it burns completely out, scatter salt in the
room and go to sleep. Make room in the jewelry box for the
goodies that Mr. Right will soon be bringing.

THE SPELL OF FOOD DELIGHTS

They say that the way to a man's heart (if he has one) is through his stomach. Here is your best bet to ensure that this little adage comes true. This is a little spice that can be used in or on anything sweet that you'll serve to your love bunny. This is not an aphrodisiac, it is a "love-o-disiac." Use with caution! And for goodness' sake, don't feed it to a party crowd unless you really want to play with fire!

You Will Need

+ some raw sugar
+ a red glass bottle or bowl
+ a little powdered cinnamon
+ a little powdered ginger

THE SPELL

On a full moon, assemble your ingredients on a table bathed
in moonlight (either outside or inside). Wear something sexy
and get really relaxed. Hold the sugar so it glistens in the
moonlight and toss a bit of it about you, saying:

> LADY OF LOVE,
> COME FROM ABOVE,
> SUGAR TO THEE,
> COME NOW TO ME!

With some of the sugar, make the sign of Venus ♀ on the
table. Place the red vessel in the circle of the Venus symbol
and put the rest of the sugar into it, saying:

> I KNOW,
> I KNOW,
> OUR LOVE
> WILL GROW!

Sweet, sweet,
Our bodies meet
From head to feet!

Add the cinnamon to the sugar, saying:

I will,
I will,
With love
I fill!
Sweet, sweet
Our bodies meet
From head to feet!

Add the ginger to the mix, and say:

Action,
Action,
I desire
Satisfaction!

SWEET, SWEET,
OUR BODIES MEET
FROM HEAD TO FEET!

Stir the mixture clockwise with your finger. As you stir,
pour all of your desires, fantasies, and feelings into it.
Dance about the concoction
three times, saying:

I KNOW, WILL, AND LOVE,
I MAKE IT REAL
BY MOONLIGHT ABOVE.
THIS SPELL I SEAL,
CONSUMATUM EST!

Sweep up the Venus symbol you made with the sugar and put it
into the container also, then seal it. When he comes over, just
add a little spice to his "apple pie" and you'll be the à la mode!

Turning a Friend into a Lover

What a pal! What a swell friend! Could he maybe, possibly become . . . something more? Are you ready to nudge that warm friendship into a smoldering romance? This little spell should do it. Just think, "Sally sells sexy seashells by the silky seashore . . . "

You Will Need
+ a small, beautiful seashell
(A found shell is best, but a bought one is fine.)
+ some of your sexiest perfume

The Spell
Take the shell and rub it all over your body, saying:

> Aphrodite from the ocean,
> Bring him now to love me,

SHELL IS FILLED BY SWEET EMOTION,
SWELLING LIKE THE SUNSET SEA,
TO ME, TO ME, TO ME!
IO EVOEE!

Keep the shell on your body, close to your skin, for a full day.
Think about him constantly. Then, on a Monday, rub a little
perfume on the shell and on yourself and say:

SHELL OF SEA,
LOVER'S VOW,
HE LUSTS FOR ME,
HE NEEDS ME NOW!
BY APHRODITE!
IO EVOEE!

At a casual yet charged moment, give him the shell and a big, big,
smile. Tell him you want him to have it because you can't forget
him. Say it is a token so he'll never forget you. He won't . . . ever.

Move In with Me Spell

The relationship is there already! Your place is perfect for both of you! So what, you wonder, is the holdup? That pesky male independent streak has simply got to be overcome. This spell is the honey that will lure that bear into your den. Try it out!

You Will Need

+ a cup or mug of his that you conveniently "borrow" but forget to return
+ some fresh soil (It's best if it is from his yard.)
+ some red nasturtium seeds

The Spell

On a Saturday night just after the new moon, set the cup in a windowsill with some of the fresh, moist soil in it. Take a pinch of the soil and scatter it to the four quarters, saying:

> Foursquare earth,
> Come what may,

COME TO MY HEARTH,
COME AND STAY!
IOPATER!

Take three of the seeds into your hand and walk in a
circle clockwise about the house, saying:

AROUND I SPIN,
EARTH AND SEED,
I DRAW HIM IN,
FULFILL MY NEED!

Plant the seeds about one inch into the cup and say:

BY SEED AND LOAM,
LEAF AND FLOWER,
I BRING HIM HOME,
BY MY POWER!
IOPATER!

Water the cup, let the seeds sprout, don't you worry,
don't you pout. As they grow, he won't sleep, soon he'll come,
for as you sow, so shall you reap!

Sweet Nothings Spell

You like it when he whispers endearments and compliments. In fact, they should be falling daily on your sacred head like rose petals, right? Nothing makes you feel as special as a few well-placed . . . words. If your honey is not silver-tongued enough, this spell will loosen that golden voice so he sings your praises. This, of course, you *always* richly deserve!

You Will Need
+ A small, cute jar with a lid
+ dried rosemary ($1/4$ cup)
+ dried rose petals ($1/2$ cup)
+ dried orange peel ($1/4$ cup)

The Spell
Place all of these ingredients into the jar. Say:

Roses for love,
Orange for heat,
Rosemary for breath,
Of words so sweet.

Then spin around fast three times, holding the open jar, saying:

I call the winds,
I call the air
Bring sweet words
And phrases fair!

Now whisper into the jar all the loving, romantic, and adoring words you long to hear. When you're done, put the lid on quickly.

The next time you see your honey, innocently give it to him as a potpourri gift and make sure that he takes a *big* sniff! Don't forget to be nice when he fawns all over you.

Taking It Back Spell

You were horrible to your sweetheart—one of your more vicious days. Oops! Hey, it happens. No use crying over spilt blood (or damaged male ego). But this time (and it is rare) you were wrong. So how to make amends without, you know, groveling? This little spell will smooth all ruffled feathers . . . and we all know that making up can be really, *really* fun.

You Will Need

+ a needle
+ blue thread
+ a new, really nice handkerchief with lots of blue in it

The Spell

On a Sunday just before the new moon, take the
needle and thread and say:

> BARBS OF GORGON
> I DID THROW;
> I DRAW THEIR STING
> AS I SEW.

Somewhere on the hanky, where it will not be seen (a hem works well), stitch six stitches in one spot, each time saying:

> HEAL THE PAIN,
> LOVE I GAIN . . .

When done, shed a tear or two for how nasty you were. Dab your kind and sorrowful eye with the hanky and say:

> BARBS BE BROKEN,
> HERE'S A TOKEN.
> GONE ALL SORROW
> BY THE MORROW!
> FELICITAS!

Give him the hanky and be contrite. It'll work like a charm—because it *is* a charm!

Call Me Spell

You wait and wait and wait. Still, that very nice, eligible, could-be-the-right-guy gentleman still hasn't called, visited, sent red roses (your favorite), or done anything to win your love! This is a very old spell that works to attract a love. It has hundreds of years of tried and true testimonials to back it up (though the phone part is new). Go for it!

You Will Need
+ a small sprig of oak with some acorns on it
+ a small sprig from an ash tree
+ an orange candle

The Spell
On a Wednesday night when the moon is waxing, take the sprigs and the candle and place them by the telephone. Light the candle and say:

ACORN CUP AND ASHEN KEY,
BID MY TRUE LOVE COME CALL ME.
BETWEEN MOONLIGHT AND FIRELIGHT,
BRING HIM OVER THE HILLS TONIGHT!

Trace a circle around the phone three times with the sprigs,
lay them under the phone, and say:

OVER THE MEADOWS, OVER THE MOOR,
OVER THE RIVERS, OVER THE SEA,
OVER THE THRESHOLD AND THROUGH MY DOOR,
CALL ME, CALL ME, CALL ME!

Put both hands on the phone and will him to call!
Finish the spell by saying:

ACORN CUP AND ASHEN KEY,
BRING MY TRUE LOVE NOW TO ME!

Don't forget to order call waiting—you don't want to miss this one!

To Resist a Love That Is Bad for You

Smart women, dumb choices. Almost every girl is a sucker for a bad guy at one time or another. This is the one time you wish you had listened to your mother. When you're hooked on a nasty guy, purge him from your system with this little spell:

You Will Need
+ a nail
+ a small cigar (It must be all-natural.)
+ a small picture of him or something of his

The Spell
Go to a crossroads at night, making sure there is at least a little earthy area nearby—even one tree will do. With the nail, scratch his name into the cigar, dig a small hole in the ground, and put the picture in it, facedown. Stab the nail through the picture and say:

Out out!
I cut you out!
To me you gave pain,
My love I regain!
Avert, avert, avert!

Light the cigar, puff it (don't inhale!), and blow the smoke to
the four directions and then into the hole. Then say:

Away, away,
I blow you away!
From my heart you fly
Far into the sky!
Avert, avert, avert!

Put the cigar completely out in the hole on the picture,
and bury the whole thing, saying:

> GONE, GONE,
> NOW YOU ARE GONE!
> AWAY FROM ME
> NOW I AM FREE!
> AVERT, AVERT AVERT!

Leave and never look back.

Spell to Make His Friends and Parents Like You (and Vice Versa)

Well, the easy part is finished—your lover thinks you are the best thing since sliced bread. (You are!) Now the real trials begin. His parents! His old pals! His relatives! I can feel the stress from here, and I don't live anywhere near you! This simple spell will make them adore you and will reveal the true, worthy, loving, and excellent sides of your sterling character that you know are within you . . . somewhere. Go out and knock 'em dead!

You Will Need

+ a small piece of white cloth
+ some rice thrown at a wedding (Make sure the couple has not divorced in the meantime!)
+ a leaf of bay laurel
+ some white thread
+ a safety pin

THE SPELL

At noon on a sunny day, assemble your items in a quiet
place in full sunlight. Smooth out the cloth on a
hard surface and say:

> EMPTY, OPEN,
> SEE IN ME ONLY GOOD.
> SO MOTE IT BE!

Put the rice on the cloth and say:

> LOVERS' CHARM,
> SAVE ME FROM HARM,
> LOVE SO FREE,
> DRAW IT TO ME!

Add the bay leaf to the rice and say:

FAIR OF FACE,
FAIR OF THOUGHT,
GRANT ME GRACE,
FEAR IS NAUGHT!

Tie the bundle together with the thread and then pin it
inside your blouse near your heart. When you feel flustered
around *them*, touch this charm and remember how wonderful
you are. Everyone will love you and they won't bother
digging into your sordid past!

Spell to Unite E-mail Lovers

E-mail, schmee-mail—words, words, words. You want to know what the guy *looks* like! It's easy to get lost in the digital wonderland, bytes of affection, chips of romance, RAM of . . . Well, you get the idea. You can still use the Internet to catch a really nice fish, but only if you know how to reel him in once he's on the cyber-hook!

THE SPELL

For seven straight days, beginning on a Friday and ending on a Thursday, send your cyber-sweetheart an e-mail. At the end of each message, add the next consecutive word in the list below (e.g., "C" the first day, "CON" the second day, "CONEC" the third day, etc.). On Thursday, end with "CONECTERE.EST." If he asks you what it means, tell him you'll explain as soon as you can meet face to face!
(*Conectere est* means "We connect now.")

C
CON

CONEC
CONECTE
CONECTERE
CONECTERE.ES
CONECTERE.EST

Each time you send one of these magical e-mails,
say the following before you hit "send":

SWIFT AS WIND,
HOT AS FIRE,
ARROW OF LOVE,
SPELL OF DESIRE,
FLY YOU FAST,
FLY YOU TRUE,
UNTIL AT LAST
I AM WITH YOU!
CONECTERE.EST!

On the Friday after the last e-mail is sent, send the whole
word-triangle at once and demand, in a loving manner, a face-
to-face meeting. You'll get your wish—after that, it's up to you!

Bad Date Cleansing Spell

What a terrible first date! No, it wasn't terrible, it was a
complete *&%ə%# disaster! It was the *Titanic* of dates! (Except,
of course, that the *Titanic* was a classy ship.) Such a date
leaves a huge psychic slime stain, like that of a giant slug
(which brings us to the cause of all this—the guy). A little
psychic "slug death" is in order. This'll clean your aura and
remove any ugly traces! Whoosh!

You Will Need
+ some salt (Sea salt or rock salt is best.)
+ a good broom
+ a dustpan

THE SPELL

First, take off all your date clothes, throw them into the
washer, and toss in some salt with the soap. Then, scatter
salt about your house or apartment, saying:

> Out tout,
> Throughout and about,
> All good come in,
> All evil stay out!

Then take a shower and place a fist-full of salt on your head.
Close your eyes. Let the salt dissolve in the water
and run down your body, saying:

> Out tout,
> Throughout and about,
> All good come in,
> All evil stay out!

Dry off and get dressed. Sweep your house, collecting all
the salt you tossed around in the dustpan. Empty the
dustpan out a window or door, saying:

OUT TOUT,
THROUGHOUT AND ABOUT,
FRIENDS COME IN,
(DATE'S NAME), STAY OUT!

He's history. . . . Anything he sends, return it with salt on it.
Forget about him, dear, go on to more enjoyable things—
like, well, *anything else!*

Spell to Forget an Old Flame

Old flames, they say, never die. The old, nostalgic memories of past romances never seem to fade, though we do tend to forget the bad parts. When the influence of an old flame lingers, when the passion of a past and long-gone love refuses to die and keeps interfering with the present, it is time to put it to rest. This spell will not eliminate the memories, but it will finally snuff the misplaced embers of a long-gone love.

You Will Need
+ nine black beans
+ a piece of black paper

The Spell
At midnight, when the moon is almost black, get the paper and the beans and sit in silence, fully remembering your old flame.

Invoke your past passion, the feelings you still hold on to.
Then, take up each bean in turn, say one line of the charm,
and put the bean onto the paper. Do this until all nine
beans are on the paper. Then fold up the paper.

Following are the nine parts of the charm to say,
one for each bean:

1. SOUL OF BLISS, PERFECT KISS, GONE . . .
2. FACE SO FAIR, GONE . . .
3. BEAUTIFUL HAIR, GONE . . .
4. ARMS SO STRONG, GONE . . .
5. LEGS SO LONG, GONE . . .
6. HEART OF FIRE, GONE . . .
7. LOINS OF DESIRE, GONE . . .
8. THOUGHTS SO FINE, GONE . . .
9. AURA DIVINE, GONE . . .

Take the bean-filled paper to a graveyard
and bury it at night. Say:

OUR LOVE WAS TRUE,
IT DID NOT LAST.
OUR LOVE IS GONE,
IT IS NOW PAST.
JOY AND PEACE
TO YOU AND I,
THE FLAME IS GONE
AND NOW: GOOD-BYE.
LETHE, LETHE, LETHE.

Spell for a Good Blind Date
(A Prince, No Frogs!)

Okay, maybe you're desperate. It seemed like a good idea at
the time—he sounded good, he's a friend of a friend, or maybe
this is a true personal-ad-why-not-give-it-a-shot kind of date,
hmm? We've all been there. This little spell *will* not guarantee
a rich, perfect, intelligent man (oxymoron!), but it will make
sure that the guy is at least . . . decent. That's worth a lot, yes?

You Will Need

+ a new pack of cheap playing cards
+ a few dried or fresh mint leaves

The Spell

From the deck, pull the jack of diamonds and the
ten of hearts. (You can toss the rest of the deck.)
Take the jack of diamonds and say:

HERE IS THE MAN OF MYSTERY,
MAKE HIM GOOD AND KIND AND FUN.
SO TONIGHT I WILL BE THE MOON,
SO TONIGHT HE WILL BE THE SUN . . .

Cover the jack with the ten of hearts and say:

GREAT AFFECTION,
GREAT ROMANCE,
GREAT ATTRACTION,
OUR HEARTS WILL DANCE!

Rub the mint on your hands, on your heart, and on the cards.
Take the cards with you on your date. Keep them in a pocket
or purse and keep them together.

If he is really great, give him the cards at the end of the date. Say
you found them and thought them a good omen. If he keeps them,
you might soon need to use the commitment spell (in this book)!

Take Me Away Spell

Home is where the heart is, and home sweet home is a great place to be, and your little love nest is lovely, but . . . you've got to get *out* sometimes, right? Not just for a movie or some Thai food, I mean, really out—out of town, maybe wa-a-a-a-y out of town! Just the two of you. A romantic safari, even if it's only to Vegas. (There's plenty of wildlife there!) Is that so much to ask? If your lover boy is being pokey and needs a push to travel, this will do it.

You Will Need

+ a piece of light blue paper
+ an orange pen or pencil
+ some lemongrass oil

THE SPELL

On a very windy Thursday morning, take your ingredients to a private place and write in the center of the paper exactly where you want to go. Be specific and mention the details of your trip if they are important.

Then fold the paper into a paper airplane, and say:

I LONG TO SEE
ANOTHER LAND,
WILLPOWER BE FREE—
BY MY HAND!

Write your name and your partner's name on the wings. Rub some lemongrass oil on the plane and on you, and say:

> BY THE WINDS OF SOUTH AND WEST,
> WE SHALL ENJOY THE VERY BEST,
> BY THE WINDS OF NORTH AND EAST,
> THIS SPELL IS SEALED AND DONE:
> RELEASED!

With a big rush, toss the paper airplane off a tall building, out a window way up high, or off a cliff—use your imagination! Say:

> I WILL TO GO.
> I WILL TO FLY.
> I CAST THIS SPELL.
> INTO THE SKY!
> CAELUS!

See a travel agent. Don't forget the sunblock!

WARDING OFF OTHER ADMIRERS OF YOUR MAN

He's great and it is a pain in the butt, right? Other women can hardly keep their hands off him. Who needs the competition? How much temptation can any man handle? (They just aren't that strong, honey!) Want to put a psychic "Do Not Touch" sign on his aura? This will do it!

YOU WILL NEED

+ some salt
+ a red pen
+ a small piece of gray paper
+ a small, inexpensive hematite stone

THE SPELL

On a new moon, sprinkle some salt about you and say:

> MOTHER OF NIGHT,
> HEAR MY PLIGHT,
> PROTECT MY MAN,
> AS BEST YOU CAN.

Take the red pen and the paper and draw a heart with his name and your name in it. Say:

> WE ARE ONE HEART,
> WE ARE ONE MIND,
> BY OUR LOVE WE'LL NEVER PART,
> MAY OUR SOULS ALWAYS BIND!

Over the heart, draw the protection rune Y and say:

THIS OUR LOVE WILL NOW PROTECT,
THIS WILL GUARANTEE RESPECT,
RIVALS FLEE
SO MOTE IT BE,
BY POWER OF THREE!

Place the hematite on the drawing and say:

WARD AND WARD AND WARD BY THREE,
SHIELDSTONE POWER MAKE IT BE.
IT IS CAST, ALL RIVALS FLEE!
GARDE!

Take the hematite and put it in a safe place. Later, hide the
paper somewhere in his clothing (a lining is best). Coats are
good, so are underwear labels . . . you get the idea. Give him
the hematite as a "good luck charm" when he goes on solo trips.
Make sure he takes it and that little lamb will never stray!

Spell for Getting Rid of Pet Peeves

He'd be perfect if only he'd . . . You know, if he would just learn to . . . I'd be so happy! Grrr-If he . . . one more time, I'll go crazy!

We've all been there, right, girls? Men are not only uncouth and barely civilized, but house-training them can take forever! This little spell will help domesticate that boy a bit—at least it'll iron out a few of the more irritating wrinkles!

You Will Need

+ a pink bar of soap that he'll use
+ a knife

The Spell

On a night when the moon is waning, take the soap and knife to a private place. Hold the soap up and say:

HERE IS HE, BONE AND FLESH.
MAY THIS SPELL MOLD AND MESH!

Hold up the knife and say:

WITH MY ANGER, WITH MY HEART
MAKE HIM CHANGE—MAKE HIM SMART!

On the soap carve the "need" rune ↑ and as you do so, yell at it about your pet peeves like you usually do. (For example, "Put the bloody toilet seat down!!")

Place the soap where he will use it, and say:

BY THIS SPELL THAT I HAVE MADE,
NOW THESE EVIL HABITS FADE,
WASH, WASH, WASH, AWAY,
BY THE NEED RUNE, SO I SAY!

You should, of course, use a different bar of soap. At least until he has washed off the rune. Things will change!

Spell to End an Office Romance

So *now* you know why everyone warns against office romances. You work together, unwind together, nature takes its course, and then—the whirlwind that comes out of nowhere can die down just as fast. Then it gets a bit sticky, no matter who opts out. (This spell gives you "Plan A" and "Plan B." If "A" doesn't work, "B" will.) Drop-kick that problem right out of your life!

You Will Need

+ a lemon
+ a new letter opener (It could have on it a symbol that fits you.)
+ an envelope

THE SPELL

On the night of the dark of the moon, near a willow or pine
tree, pierce the lemon with the letter opener, saying:

> OUR MATING IS OVER,
> LET IT BE SEALED,
> NO LONGER LOVERS,
> NOTHING'S REVEALED . . .

Pull the letter opener out of the lemon, bury the
lemon at the foot of the tree, and say:

> TREE ROOTS COVER,
> EARTH HIDE THE PAIN,
> NO LONGER MY LOVER,
> OUR BALANCE REGAIN!
> METIS!

Give him the letter opener as a peace offering. See how
the "Let's return to being friends" stage works. If he proceeds
to be a pain in the neck or obnoxiously heartbroken
(or if you are), proceed to Plan B. Dig up the lemon. Take some
of the peel, put it into the envelope, and send it to some
far-away city. (Don't put a return address on it.)
Write his name and *Hold for pickup at this post office* on the
front. When you send it, repeat the last verse of the spell
again, but change the fourth line to:

BEGONE, YOU ARE PAIN!

He'll soon be transferred . . . or whatever. Then, just
wash that man right out of your hair!

Making Beautiful Music Together

Ah, romance. There is simply not enough of it in the world today. If there is not enough romance in your particular corner of the world, try this little spell to add that special exotic energy to an already okay relationship, or even to help get a new one off on the right foot.

You Will Need
+ a new music CD or cassette
+ sandalwood incense
+ sandalwood oil
+ hot pink or magenta paper

The Spell
Choose a really romantic CD that you know for a fact your guy will like, but choose one he doesn't own. On a Friday night,

open the CD, light the incense, put some sandalwood oil on
your naked body and have as much fun as one person can
have alone (use your imagination) while clutching the CD
to your heart, saying:

> SOUND OF LOVE,
> LOVE OF SOUND,
> BRING IT THROUGH,
> BRING IT ROUND.
> EROS AUDIERE!

Mark the top of the CD case with a pentagram using the
oil and some of your sweat, then pass it through the
incense smoke and say:

> FULL OF LUST, LOVE, AND LIGHT,
> MUSIC OF THE HEART FLY FREE,
> FILL US ALL WITH JOY AND MIGHT,
> AS WE LISTEN, MAY IT BE!

Wrap the CD in the pink paper and give it to him. Make sure
that you listen to it the first time together. And, of course,
wear a little of the sandalwood oil as well.
Hit the "repeat play" button.
Grrrrr! Make some beautiful music together!

About the Author

Sophia is a professional psychic and spiritual teacher with more than twenty years of experience, both in the U.S. and abroad. Part Native American, she was taught how to tap her psychic powers by her grandparents when she was a child. From the age of three, she learned psychic reading, card reading, coffee-ground reading, astrology, and other forms of divination. She is also a professional photographer. Her previous book, *Fortunetelling with Playing Cards*, was published in 1996. *The Sophia Deck of Fortunetelling Cards* will be published in 1997.